Animal Farm Classroom Questions

A SCENE BY SCENE TEACHING GUIDE

Amy Farrell

SCENE BY SCENE
ENNISKERRY, IRELAND

Copyright © 2015 by Amy Farrell.

All rights reserved. No part of this publication may be reproduced, distributed or transmitted in any form or by any means, including photocopying, recording, or other electronic or mechanical methods, without the prior written permission of the publisher, except in the case of brief quotations embodied in critical reviews and certain other noncommercial uses permitted by copyright law. For permission requests, write to the publisher, addressed "Attention: Permissions Coordinator," at the address below.

Scene by Scene
11 Millfield, Enniskerry
Wicklow, Ireland.
www.scenebysceneguides.com

Animal Farm Classroom Questions/Amy Farrell. —1st ed.
ISBN 978-1-910949-10-8

Contents

Chapter One	1
Chapter Two	3
Chapter Three	5
Chapter Four	6
Chapter Five	7
Chapter Six	9
Chapter Seven	11
Chapter Eight	14
Chapter Nine	16
Chapter Ten	18

Chapter One

1. What is your first impression of Mr. Jones?

2. Why is there a "stirring and fluttering" throughout the farm?

3. Describe Major, the pig.

4. Describe Boxer, the cart-horse.

5. Describe Benjamin, the donkey.

6. Describe the scene in the barn as the animals prepare for their meeting.

7. Who is the only creature to miss the meeting?

8. What message does Major have for the assembled animals about their lives?

9. What does Major have to say about Man?
   Is there truth in what he says?

10. According to Major, what fate awaits the cows, pigs, hens, sheep, horses and dogs? Is this true?

11. Major calls the animals "comrades". What does this word mean? What is the effect of Major using this term?

12. What does Major wish to achieve by having a rebellion?

13. Major tells the animals, "All men are enemies. All animals are comrades." Is this a powerful message, in your opinion?

14. What does Major warn against, "in fighting against Man"?

15. What are the main points in Major's message? If you were one of the animals listening to this speech, how would you react to these ideas?

16. "The singing of this song threw the animals into the wildest excitement." Why do they react like this, do you think?

17. How does the last paragraph in this chapter add to your impression of Mr. Jones?

Chapter Two

1. What effect did Major's speech have on the animals?

2. Why did teaching and organising the others fall to the pigs?

3. Describe the young boars, Snowball and Napoleon.

4. What is Squealer like?

5. What is Animalism?

6. The pigs' teachings are met with resistance at first. What arguments do the other animals put forward? Are these sensible arguments, in your view?

7. Mollie, the white mare, is concerned about having sugar and wearing ribbons after the Rebellion. What information does Snowball give her on these issues?

8. What "lies" does Moses spread? What could the author be referring to here?

9. What makes Boxer and Clover such "faithful disciples"?

10. What kind of farmer is Mr. Jones?

11. What brings about the "Rebellion'?

12. How do the men react to the animals' uprising?

13. After they claim Manor Farm, what do the animals do first?

14. How do the animals react to the farmhouse?

15. What "resolution" do they agree about the farmhouse?

16. What are the seven commandments of Animalism? What is your response to these rules?

17. What is the mood on the farm as the chapter ends?

18. From what we have read so far, what different types of people could the different animals represent?

Chapter Three

1. Can the animals manage the farm successfully?

2. "…every animal down to the humblest worked…"
   What is significant about this?

3. What sort of worker is Boxer?
   Are you impressed by his work ethic?

4. Has life improved without Mr. Jones, the farmer? Explain.

5. What happens on Sundays?

6. Are the pigs good leaders? Explain your view.

7. How successful are the animals at learning to read?

8. What is the 'essential principle' of Animalism?

9. How do Snowball's and Napoleon's views on education differ?

10. At the end of the chapter, Squealer tells the other animals that apples and milk are essential to the pigs' well-being. What is your reaction to his arguments here?

11. Are all animals treated equally as the chapter ends?

Chapter Four

1. How has Mr. Jones spent his time since the rebellion?

2. Are other farmers sympathetic towards him?

3. What propaganda is spread by the neighbouring farmers about Animal Farm?
   Why do they do this?
   Are these rumours successful?

4. How do the Animals defend the farm when Mr. Jones tries to take it back? Are they brave here? Are you shocked by their violence?

5. What makes Boxer so upset here?

6. What is your response to the animals' decision to create a military decoration?

7. What will Mr. Jones' gun be used for?
   Why is this significant?

Chapter Five

1. How is Mollie being "troublesome"?

2. Are you surprised that she leaves Animal Farm?

3. Why do the animals never mention her again?

4. What problems are caused by Snowball and Napoleon?

5. How does Napoleon undermine Snowball?

6. What does Snowball's windmill plan involve?

7. How does Napoleon let Snowball know what he thinks of his plans for the windmill?

8. How is the farm divided on the issue of the windmill? Can you see the point of view of each side?

9. Why do the animals fear another attempt to recapture the farm is likely?

10. Do you think the constant opposition between Snowball and Napoleon is harmless or damaging to Animal Farm?

11. What is your response to Napoleon releasing the dogs on Snowball?

12. "…They wagged their tails to him in the same way as the other dogs had been used to do to Mr. Jones." What is significant about this line? Is this in keeping with 'Animalism', do you think?

13. What changes will be made to Sunday morning Meetings with Napoleon in charge? Comment on this.

14. What prevents the other animals from speaking up against Napoleon?

15. After the meeting, what does Squealer do?

16. How does Squealer speak of Snowball? Why does he do this?

17. In what different ways are the animals controlled by Napoleon and the pigs?

18. At this point, are the animals better off than they were before the rebellion?

19. Are you surprised to learn that Napoleon intends to build the windmill after all?

20. Why do the animals accept what Squealer says about Snowball and the windmill? Does this surprise you?

Chapter Six

1. Describe life on Animal Farm at this point.

2. What problems do the animals face, building the windmill?

3. What motivates Boxer to work so hard?

4. What prompts Napoleon to decide that the animals will engage in trade?

5. Why does the idea of trade make the other animals uneasy?

6. What are your views on whether or not they should engage in trade?

7. What prevents discussions and disagreements at Meetings with Napoleon in charge?

8. How would you describe Squealer's role on the farm?

9. What attitude do the humans have towards the farm? Is the author making a political comment here, do you think?

10. What is significant about the pigs moving into the farm house?
    Are Squealer's reasons for this move convincing, in your opinion?

11. What do you notice about the Fourth Commandment here? What is happening?

12. Why does Squealer always suggest that Jones will return if the pigs aren't treated as they decree? What is your reaction to this?

13. "…the windmill compensated for everything…"
    What is the windmill coming to symbolise for the animals?

14. What is Napoleon's reaction to the destruction of the windmill?

15. Comment on Napoleon pronouncing the death sentence on Snowball.

16. Are the animals too gullible here, in the way they accept Snowball's guilt without question?

17. From what you have read so far, what political or historical parallels have you noticed between the story and real events?

Chapter Seven

1. How much notice are the animals of Animal Farm paying to the outside world?

2. "Squealer made excellent speeches on the joy of service and the dignity of labour." Comment on this line.

3. What problems are the animals facing?

4. What lies are humans spreading about Animal Farm? Why are they doing this, do you think?

5. How is Napoleon combatting these lies?

6. "For the first time since the expulsion of Jones there was something resembling a rebellion."
What has caused this dissent?
Do you sympathise with the hens?

7. "Napoleon acted swiftly and ruthlessly."
What do you think of how he forces the hens to comply here?

8. Is Napoleon a good leader, in your opinion?

9. "Whenever anything went wrong it became usual to attribute it to Snowball."
Are you surprised that the animals fall for this?

10. What do Squealer's 'secret documents' reveal?
What is your reaction to this?

11. What makes Squealer's version of events so convincing, time and again?

12. Would it be fair to call Squealer's tales propaganda? Explain your view.

13. "…we have reason to think that some of Snowball's secret agents are lurking among us at this moment!"
Is this really the case? What is going on here?

14. When Napoleon's dogs attack Boxer, he naively assumes it was a mistake. What do you think is going on here?

15. Why do the four pigs confess that they are in league with Snowball? Do you believe their guilt?

16. Why do other animals confess, in your view?

17. "They, too, were slaughtered."
What is your reaction to this?

18. What effect do these executions have on the assembly?

19. Boxer is deeply troubled by the situation on the farm. What is his solution to improve their plight?

20. Why do Clover's eyes fill with tears as she looks at the farm? How has it come to this?

21. "Whatever happened she would remain faithful."
Why doesn't Clover rebel here?

22. Why has the song, 'Beasts of England', been abolished, according to Squealer?
Why did Napoleon ban the song, in your opinion?

Chapter Eight

1. What has happened the Sixth Commandment?

2. What special treatment does Napoleon receive on the farm? What is your reaction to this special treatment?

3. What are relations like between Animal Farm and the neighbouring farms at this stage?

4. What is Snowball alleged to have done to the seed corn? What is your reaction to Squealer's lies about Snowball?

5. "The pigs were in ecstasies over Napoleon's cunning." Has Napoleon been crafty here?

6. "When captured, he said, Frederick should be boiled alive." Is Napoleon's reaction understandable?

7. How do the animals fare when the next attack comes?

8. What happens to the windmill?
   Why did Frederick's men do this, do you think?

9. "They had won, but they were weary and bleeding." If you were an animal on the farm, how would you feel at this stage?

10. Squealer interprets the outcome of the battle as a victory. Why is Boxer slow to agree with him?

11. What happens when the pigs discover a case of whisky?

12. What has happened to the Fifth Commandment?

13. In you opinion, are the animals any better off now, than they were when Jones ran the farm?

Chapter Nine

1. Are you hopeful regarding Boxer's retirement? Explain your view.

2. The pigs and dogs receive greater rations than the other animals. What is your response to this?

3. "…doubtless it had been worse in the old days." Is this the case? Why do you think this is so?

4. The piglets receive preferential treatment. What comment is Orwell making here about equality?

5. Are the pigs 'wealthier' than the other animals? Explain your answer.

6. What makes up for the "hardships to be borne"? Would this make up for the hardships, for you?

7. Why do the animals enjoy the Spontaneous Demonstrations?

8. What might Moses the Raven and his talk of Sugarcandy Mountain represent in the story?

9. How is Boxer deteriorating with age?

10. "There lay Boxer, between the shafts of the cart…"
    Comment on this image.

11. "They're taking Boxer away!" Why does Benjamin cause an outcry when the van comes for Boxer?

12. What is your reaction to the pigs' treatment of Boxer here?

13. Napoleon is still using Boxer, even in death.
    Do you agree with this statement? Explain your point of view.

14. Where, do you think, did the pigs get the money for another case of whisky?

15. In what different ways do the pigs control the other animals on the farm? Why are they able to do this?

Chapter Ten

1. "…in fact no animal had ever actually retired." What is your response to this?

2. What is the windmill being used for?

3. What is life like for the majority of animals?

4. Are all animals equal on Animal Farm?

5. The animals feel a sense of "honour and privilege in being members of Animal Farm." Are they right to feel like this, in your opinion?

6. What is significant about the new chant Squealer has taught to the sheep?

7. What has replaced the Seven Commandments on the barn wall? What is your reaction to this?

8. What is your reaction to the human-like behaviour of the pigs?

9. Mr. Pilkington of Foxwood describes Animal Farm as "a farm owned and operated by pigs." Does this surprise you?

10. Why does Mr. Pilkington congratulate the pigs on their treatment of the other farm animals?

11. What changes to the farm's routine does Napoleon announce to the pigs and men?

12. What is happening as the novel ends? How do you feel about this? Is this an optimistic or pessimistic ending?

13. How did the pigs use their intelligence in this story?

14. What went wrong for the animals on Animal Farm? What prevented them from achieving their ideals?

15. Comment on the imagery and symbolism in this novel.

16. Do you think Orwell really intended this to be "A Fairy Story"?

17. What, if anything, saddens you about this story?

18. What did you like about this novel?

WWW.SCENEBYSCENEGUIDES.COM

Visit www.scenebysceneguides.com to see our full catalogue of Classroom Questions and Workbooks.

Hamlet Scene by Scene Classroom Questions

Romeo and Juliet Scene by Scene Classroom Questions

King Lear Scene by Scene Classroom Questions

Macbeth Scene by Scene Classroom Questions

A Doll's House Classroom Questions

Animal Farm Classroom Questions

Foster Classroom Questions

Good Night, Mr. Tom Classroom Questions

WWW.SCENEBYSCENEGUIDES.COM

Subscribe to our newsletter to keep up to date with all the latest title releases at www.scenebysceneguides.com/newsletter

Martyn Pig Classroom Questions

Of Mice and Men Classroom Questions

Pride and Prejudice Classroom Questions

Private Peaceful Classroom Questions

The Fault in Our Stars Classroom Questions

The Old Man and the Sea Classroom Questions

The Outsiders Classroom Questions

To Kill a Mockingbird Classroom Questions

The Spinning Heart Classroom Questions

www.ingramcontent.com/pod-product-compliance
Lightning Source LLC
Chambersburg PA
CBHW070120110526
44587CB00016BA/2741